For three courageous brothers—
Talon, Ruben, and Beau
• Carla •

To Seren
and Elsie, who
love outdoor
adventures.
• Cath •

Let's Play Outdoors!
Exploring Nature for Children

Illustrated by Carla McRae
Written by Catherine Ard

This book was conceived, edited and designed by gestalten.

Edited by Robert Klanten, Maria-Elisabeth Niebius, and Amber Jones

Design and layout by Constanze Hein, Book Book

Research by Polly Jarman

Typefaces: Euclid Flex by Swiss Typefaces, FF Providence Sans Pro by FontFont

Printed by Gutenberg Beuys Feindruckerei GmbH, Langenhagen
Made in Germany

Published by Little Gestalten, Berlin 2020
978-3-89955-843-2

The German edition is available under ISBN 978-3-89955-842-5

For more information, and to order books, please visit www.little.gestalten.com

Bibliographic information published by the Deutsche Nationalbibliothek.
The Deutsche Nationalbibliothek lists this publication in the Deutsche
Nationalbibliografie; detailed bibliographic data are available online at www.dnb.de

This book was printed on paper certified according to the standards of the FSC®

FSC
www.fsc.org

MIX
Paper from
responsible sources
FSC® C009051

Let's Play Outdoors!

Exploring Nature for Children

Illustrated by Carla McRae
Written by Catherine Ard

LITTLE
GESTALTEN

Wild Adventures

Are you ready to explore the great outdoors? Whether you are visiting a wood or a park, or just playing in your back garden, there is plenty to discover all through the year. So grab your bag, a sun or rain hat, some of your friends, and go explore the wild outdoors!

How to Use This Book

In this book, you'll discover great ideas for things to make, learn, and do outside.

Find a notebook you like and use it for ideas of things to write and draw when you are out and about. Look out for the notebook icon in this book.

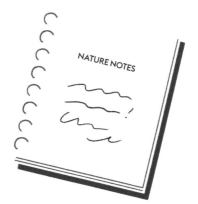

NATURE NOTES

These wildlife icons will give you tips on how to keep yourself and other animals safe.

Now wash your grubby hands!

Tweet! Ask an adult to help you.

Watch out for sharp objects on the ground.

Do not put anything in your mouth—it might be poisonous!

Take Care

Follow these tips to stay safe outdoors:

- Always have a grown-up with you.
- Grown-ups are in charge of lighting campfires, cooking, and using any tools.
- Wear shoes with grip and be careful on uneven, wet, and slippery surfaces.
- In some countries wild animals can be dangerous. Find out about the local wildlife before you go on a nature hunt or camping.

Be Prepared

Before you set off, pack all the things you need for your outdoor adventure. Don't forget to check the weather! Is it hot, wet, or cold outside? Make sure you have the right clothes to keep you warm, safe, clean, and dry.

Empty Bag for Collecting Objects

Magnifying Glass

Sunhat

Sunglasses

Suncream

Snacks

Waterproof Coat

Pencil

Notebook

Bottle of Water

Sturdy Shoes or Boots

Rucksack

Warm Clothes

9

Caring for Nature

STOMP! SMASH! CRASH! Here come the giants, squashing everything with their huge hands and feet! Don't be a clumsy giant on your wild adventures—learn how to share the outdoors with all living things, great and small.

Save Our Homes

Don't pick flowers or plants, break off branches, or remove any rotting wood. Nuts, flowers, leaves, trees, and berries provide food and homes for insects and animals.

PICK ON SOMEONE YOUR OWN SIZE!

Don't Be a Litter Bug

Put all your rubbish in a bin or take it home. Wrappers and packets won't rot and can harm wildlife. Even apple cores and banana skins are harmful in a place where they don't grow naturally. Always leave the wild place exactly as you found it.

Keep Off the Grass

When you are out walking, stick to the paths so that you don't trample on weeds and wildflowers or crush grasses and plants.

Shut the Gate

Obey any signs you see in the countryside. Walk quietly and calmly across fields where farm animals are kept so you don't scare them. Keep your distance and always close gates behind you.

RIGHTS FOR INSECTS!

Do Not Disturb

Remember that you share the outdoors you are exploring with lots of other creatures. Give them space, and don't trample, kick, or poke their homes.

11

Nature Detectives

Nature is everywhere! You can hear it, see it, touch it, and smell it all through the year. Even a bustling city is bursting with birdsong. Step outside, open your eyes and ears, and get ready to explore with your fingers and nose!

Listen!

What can you hear when you walk down the street? Listen out for tweeting birds, rustling leaves, pattering rain, and buzzing bees.

Count all the different bird calls. Can you copy them?

Smell!

Take a deep breath. Ahhhh! What can you smell? Freshly cut grass or damp autumn leaves? Pine needles or sweet herbs and flowers wafting on the breeze?

Sniff out different smells on your walk to school. Where are they coming from? Do they smell sweet, woody, fresh, or fruity?

See!

Look up, look down, and all around. There's a rainbow of colors to see in the sky and on plants and trees. Watch things on the move, from great drifting clouds to tiny windblown seeds.

Can you spot five different things that are green?

Touch!

Take your fingers on a treasure hunt. How many different textures can they feel? Discover rough bark and polished pebbles, fuzzy moss and velvety petals.

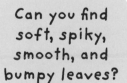

Can you find soft, spiky, smooth, and bumpy leaves?

Do not put anything in your mouth!

Window Camera

Create an easy-peasy camera to watch the world through. It doesn't click and you can't keep the pictures, but peep through its cardboard window and you will notice all sorts of natural wonders.

You will need:

- A ruler and a pen
- A piece of cardboard (such as an old cereal box)
- A pair of scissors

1. Use a ruler to draw a square in the middle of your piece of cardboard. Make sure you have a border outside the square.

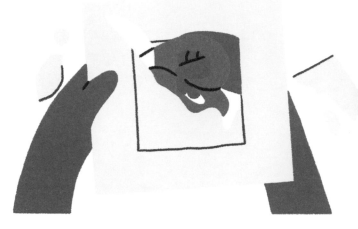

2. Pierce a hole in the middle of the cardboard with scissors, then cut around the inside of the square to make a window.

3. Grab your window camera, a notebook, and a pen, and go outside. Hold your camera up to anything interesting that you see.

4. Lots of wild things grow in towns and cities. Seek out plants pushing up through pavements and wildflowers on walls.

Look up through the trees and zoom in on the ground. There is something to find, no matter where you point your camera.

TWEET! TWEET!

Try using your camera to look closely at plants or insects.

- Make a list of the birds, insects, and minibeasts that you find.
- Draw a map of where you found each one.
- Sketch a view seen through your camera.

Can you spot any trails of ants moving around?

What magical cloud creatures can you spot in the sky?

On the Move

Sometimes clouds whizz across the sky and other times they drift slowly by. Watch the clouds to see which way the wind is blowing. You can also lick the tip of your finger and hold it up. The side that feels coolest is the direction that the wind is coming from.

Cloud Watching

Look out for
these cloud shapes:

- Wispy strands
- Small rows, like fish scales
- Fluffy clouds with flat bottoms
- Tall, dark, towering
clouds

Rain or Shine

White, fluffy clouds mean the
weather will be fine. Gray or black
clouds are full of water and mean
it could be about to rain.

If it's sunny
wear your
sunglasses, and
never look
directly at the
sun.

Did you know you can see animal shapes in the clouds?
Choose a safe, comfortable place, lie down, and gaze up at
the sky. Different shapes of clouds pass by almost every day.

17

Forest Rattles

Shake it up with an easy-to-make instrument! These fun and colorful rattles are great for making music outside. They are created from bits and bobs you can find in nature and around your home.

You will need:

- A Y-shaped stick
- Some string or wool
- Any found objects with a hole in the middle—beads, buttons, shells, nuts, seeds

1. Choose a small, Y-shaped stick. You will create your rattle in the space between the arms of the Y.

2. Tie your string to one arm of the Y with a double knot. Leave enough loose string so that it can easily reach the other arm.

Remember, don't pick anything that is growing and don't eat anything you find.

3. Thread your found objects onto the string. Tie the string around the other arm of the Y with a double knot.

4. You can now shake out a rhythm with your forest rattle. Get your friends to make their own and form a woodland band.

Insect Inspection

Search the ground to find where minibeasts are hiding. They might be crawling, slithering, burrowing, or beetling among leaves and rotting logs.

You will need:

- A magnifying glass or a pot with a magnifying-glass lid

- A small spoon

Lots of minibeasts live under rocks. Find a big stone on the ground and turn it over.

How many different creatures can you see?

Soft and rotten wood is called deadwood. It is home to all sorts of insects. Search the nooks and hollows in old logs, or lift up a fallen branch and look underneath to find bugs.

Using your spoon, gently lift up the bugs so you can inspect them more closely with a magnifying glass. Can you see their feelers and mouth parts? How many legs can you count?

Build a Bug Hotel

Make a tiny woodland shelter and fill it with creature comforts, then wait for the minibeasts to move in!

1. Gather sticks, bark, feathers, stones, and any other things you find on the ground.

2. Choose a shady spot to start building, such as the base of a tree trunk.

3. Make a shelter from the twigs and leaves. Fill the inside with stone stools and make feathery beds.

What's the difference between a centipede and a millipede?

A centipede has one pair of legs on each body segment. A millipede has two.

We Need Bees!

Bees are important insects, they have a big job to do. Many of the fruit and vegetables that we eat could not have grown without their help.

Flowering plants and trees hum with bees drinking their sweet juice, called nectar. Bees also collect and eat pollen from flowers. Pollen is a sticky powder that plants need to make seeds.

Honeybees are champion pollen collectors because the powder sticks to the little hairs on their legs.

As they fly from flower to flower, the pollen from one rubs off onto another. This is called pollination.

When this happens, seeds can form. Many plant seeds grow inside fruit or vegetables.

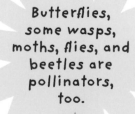

Butterflies, some wasps, moths, flies, and beetles are pollinators, too.

Bees in Trouble

The wild places where bees and butterflies live and feed are being cut down to make space for new houses or crops.

Some crops are sprayed with chemicals that make plants grow bigger but also make bees and insects sick.

Go Wild for Bees!

Here's how to get your area buzzing:

- Find out which wildflowers are good for bees and butterflies, and sow some seeds in your garden or in window pots.

- Ask your school if you can plant some wildflowers in the school's outdoor area.

- Plant tall grasses or let a patch of lawn grow long. This gives bees a shady place to take a break from feeding and flying.

- Make a bug hotel, or leave logs to rot in your garden. They make great places for bees and butterflies to shelter.

- Tell grown-ups not to spray plants with bug-killing chemicals.

Put a shallow dish of water out for thirsty bees and butterflies.

23

Bark Rubbings

Tree bark has ridges and swirls, a bit like your fingerprints. Head for some trees with paper and crayons and make some colorful patterns appear before your eyes!

You will need:

- Crayons (wrappers removed)
- Paper

1. Start by choosing a tree. Try to find one that has interesting textures on its bark.

2. Hold your piece of paper up against the trunk. Using the long edge of the crayon, gently rub across the paper.

3. The markings of the bark will appear on your paper. Each type of tree has a different pattern. How many can you find?

What other surfaces have unusual textures?
You could make a rubbing of a tree's leaf to go with its bark rubbing.
How about taking a rubbing of different rocks and stones, too?
• Make a list of all the trees you can name.
• Write words to describe the bark. Is it rough, smooth, lumpy, or bumpy?

Outdoor Dens

Who needs a tent when you can make a shelter among the trees? A den is the perfect place to watch wildlife from, shelter from the rain, and hang out with friends.

You will need:

- Rope
- A tarpaulin, old sheets, or blankets
- Rocks

1. Find two trees with slim trunks that are close together.

2. Tie one end of the rope around one tree. Tie the rope above a bump in the bark to stop it slipping down.

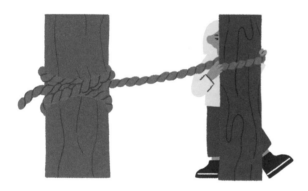

3. Pull the long end of the rope across to the other tree and tie it at the same height.

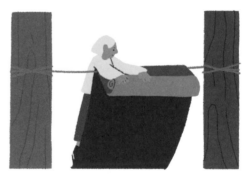

4. Hang your tarpaulin, sheet or blankets over the rope.

Take down your den before you leave and take man-made things home with you.

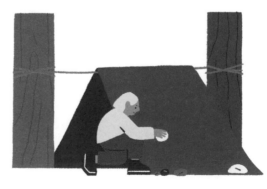

5. Pull out the sides and weigh them down with rocks.

Weatherproof Walls

You can make your den windproof and rainproof by using branches. Weave thin branches between thicker ones, then put them in the ground. Cover the branches with leaves or mud. This will make your den hard to spot, too!

Campfires

A campfire is an important part of any camp. Even more important is to know how to set one up safely, so that it is not dangerous for you, for animals, or for surrounding nature. Get help from an adult and follow the steps on this page. Once it's lit, you can keep warm, cook a meal, and see by its flickering light at night.

You will need:

- Tinder, kindling, and firewood
- A fire-retardant glove
- Cotton wool balls (optional)
- A flint-and-steel tool
- A big bucket of water

Make sure you are allowed to gather firewood where you are camping.

Don't start a fire in windy or hot, dry weather, as fires spread quickly.

Many national parks, forests, and public spaces do not allow fires, so check first.

Always keep a safe distance from the fire. Never leave it unattended.

Search on the ground for dry grass, pine needles, and thin bark strips to serve as **tinder** to start the fire.

Gather two handfuls of pine cones, dry leaves, and twigs as **kindling** to get the fire going. The twigs should be as thick as a pencil.

Pine Needles

Pine Cones

Bark Strips

Twigs

Dry Grass

Leaves

For **firewood**, gather a pile of sticks as thick as your thumb and a pile of branches as thick as your wrist.

Lighting a Campfire

A grown-up needs to be present the whole time!

1. Find a flat area away from tents and overhanging trees. Sweep away any twigs and leaves.

2. Make a **square** around your clearing with four thick branches. This will keep your fire from spreading.

3. Have your firewood and fire-retardant glove ready and a bucket of water to put out the fire.

4. Pull a few cotton wool balls apart (if using) and add them to a small pile of tinder. Surround this with kindling.

Put out the fire with the bucket of water when you have finished.

5. Use the flint-and-steel tool to make a spark and set light to the tinder.

6. When the flames are flickering, slowly add more kindling, then the smallest pieces of firewood first.

29

Campfire Stories

There is something special and magical about a campfire. Gather everyone safely around the warm, flickering flames so you can all sing songs, tell stories, or close your eyes and relax.

For thousands of years, people have sat around campfires to talk and listen. They have passed down legends about people and places from the past and told tales of good spirits and spooky ghosts.

Enjoy a Campfire Singsong

Why don't you sing some songs around the fire? Pick a tune everyone knows and make up your own words to sing together.

Team up to Tell a Story

The first person begins with a sentence, then the person to the left repeats the sentence and adds one of their own. The next person has to remember both sentences and add their own, and so on. It could become a long tall tale with lots of twists and turns!

Can you invent a funny, magical, or mysterious story inspired by your own adventures?

Outdoor Cooking

Food tastes so much better when you eat it outside in the fresh air! Satisfy rumbling tummies with these tasty recipes that can be cooked on a barbecue or a campsite fire.

Take all uneaten food and rubbish home with you.

You will need:

- Medium potatoes
- Olive oil
- Fork
- Tinfoil
- Tongs
- Heat-proof glove
- Butter
- Knife

Smoking Hot Potatoes

1. Rub the potato skins with a little olive oil. Use a fork to stab some holes in the potatoes so the steam can escape when they cook, then wrap them in tinfoil.

2. Ask a grown-up to place the potatoes on the barbecue or in the campfire embers using tongs. Leave for 20 minutes, then turn and leave for another 20 minutes.

3. Ask a grown-up to remove the potatoes from the heat with a heatproof glove. Squeeze them to make sure they are soft.

4. Leave to cool for five minutes, then cut open, add a knob of butter, and dig in!

Always ask a grown-up to place food on and remove it from the barbecue or fire.

Campfire Bread Twirls

You will need:

- Sticks
- 1 cup all-purpose flour
- 2 tsps baking powder
- 1 tsp salt
- Mixing bowl
- Sugar to taste
- ¼ cup olive oil
- ⅔ cup water

1. Find some sticks about as long as your arm and as thick as two fingers. Wash off any dirt or leaves.

2. Put the flour, baking powder, sugar, and salt in a bowl, then mix in the olive oil and water to make a dough.

3. Roll the dough into six thin sausages. Wrap a piece of dough around each stick, starting from one end, then squeeze the ends of the dough in place.

4. Hold your stick over a barbecue or campfire embers, not the flame. Keep turning it while the bread bakes.

5. When it is golden brown, take the bread off the stick. You could dip it in something tasty!

Stargazing

Lie on a blanket on a clear night and look up at the twinkling stars. Some groups of stars make patterns when they are joined together by invisible lines. These are called constellations.

Can you find these constellations in the scene?

• Cygnus (a swan)

• Scorpius (a scorpion)

• Leo (a lion)

You can download star maps of your area, or use a phone app to help you spot constellations and planets.

The Big Dipper is part of a large constellation called the Great Bear. The seven bright stars in it look like a saucepan. Can you also see the bear's head and legs?

Can you spot huge holes on the moon's surface?

These are called craters. They are made by space rocks crashing onto the moon.

Can you spot a shooting star?

The light from a shooting star you see streaking across the sky is actually rock and dust speeding through space. When it travels through the air that surrounds Earth, it burns up, making the bright light that we see.

Tree ID

Some trees are thin and pointy, while others are wide and leafy. Some grow in thick, steamy jungles, others stand alone in dry deserts. There are so many different types of trees, but they do have lots of things in common.

Deciduous Trees

These trees shed their leaves to store up energy for cold or dry weather. In cooler parts of the world this happens in fall. In warm parts it happens during the dry season.

All trees have roots, a trunk, bark, branches, twigs, and leaves. Can you find each part on this tree?

Lovely Leaves

You can spot deciduous trees by getting to know the shape of their leaves. Most have flat and wide leaves.

Thirsty Roots

A tree's roots stop it from falling over. They also suck up the water and goodness from the soil that a tree needs to grow.

Evergreen Trees

These trees are covered with leaves all year round. Their leaves are often thin and pointy, like needles.

- Draw some trees that you see. Can you label the parts?
- Look for trees with fruit, cones, and nuts.

Super Seeds

There are lots of different types of seeds. The stone inside a cherry, the conker inside its shell, and the scales in a pine cone are all seeds. Some seeds even have wings that help them to drift on the wind!

Tree Climbing

What can you see from up in a tree? Climb up through the branches on a calm, dry day and find a perch, then peer through the leaves and take a look.

Tweet! Never climb trees that have nests or beehives.

Pick your kit:

- Shoes with grip, like sneakers, not boots or slip-ons that slide off!
- Clothes that won't catch on branches.

Find the Perfect Tree!

You will need to look for:

- Evenly spaced branches all the way up.
- A strong, upright trunk, not one that is leaning or hollow.
- Solid branches—avoid ones that are cracked or rotten.
- Soft ground underneath.
- Check for stinging plants and sharp objects on the ground.

Start climbing!

Follow these tips to become a top climber:

- **Look** upwards when you climb up, and downwards when climbing down.
- **Stand** on thick branches near the trunk, where they are **strongest**.
- **Test** each branch before you put your full weight on it.
- **Find** knots, holes, and lumps in the bark where you can place your hands and feet.
- **Touch** the tree with two hands and a leg, or two legs and a hand, at all times.
- **Keep** your hands free for climbing.
- **Remember** your route up and come down the same way.
- **Take** it slowly as you go up!

Don't climb too high—make sure an adult can always reach you.

Ask a grown-up to stay with you while you climb.

Tree Stories

Did you know that every tree has the story of its life written right through its center? Find a tree stump and learn to read its rings!

Growing Older

Every year a tree grows another layer of bark around its trunk. These layers are the rings that you can see in a tree stump.

Trees can live for thousands of years! The oldest tree is more than 5,000 years old!

I'm going to count my rings!

This ring is the tree's first year.

Mmmm! The older the better.

Count the Rings

Each ring has a light part and a dark part. One ring marks a year of growing in the tree's life. You can count the rings to find out how old the tree was.

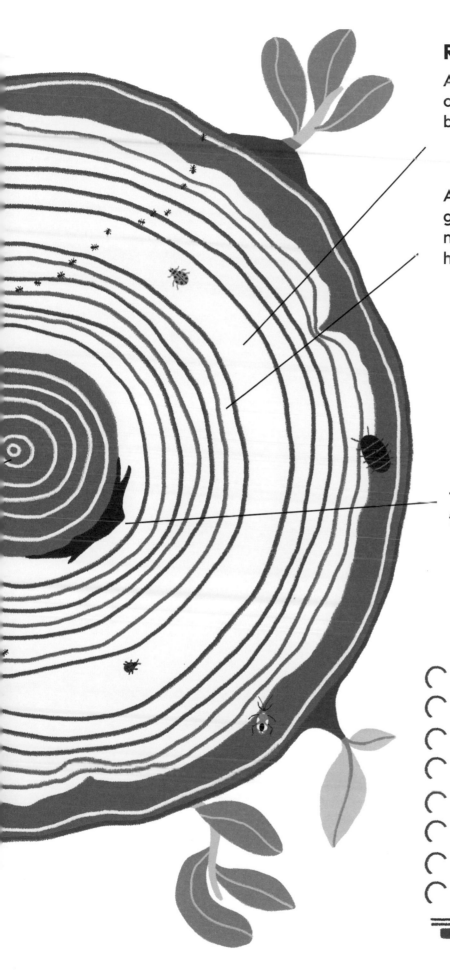

Read the Story

A wide ring means the tree grew a lot that year. There must have been plenty of sun and rain.

A narrow ring means the tree did not grow much. Perhaps it was too dry or not very sunny that year. Or maybe hungry bugs ate lots of its leaves.

This black scar is where a forest fire burned the tree one year.

- Whenever you see a tree stump, have a go at counting the rings.
- Write down the age of each one you find.

41

Animal Trails

Some wild animals come out at night and others hide when humans are near. Discover what creatures have passed your way by following the trail of clues.

Animal Footprints

It's easier to spot animal tracks on muddy or snowy ground. Have you seen any of these tracks near you?

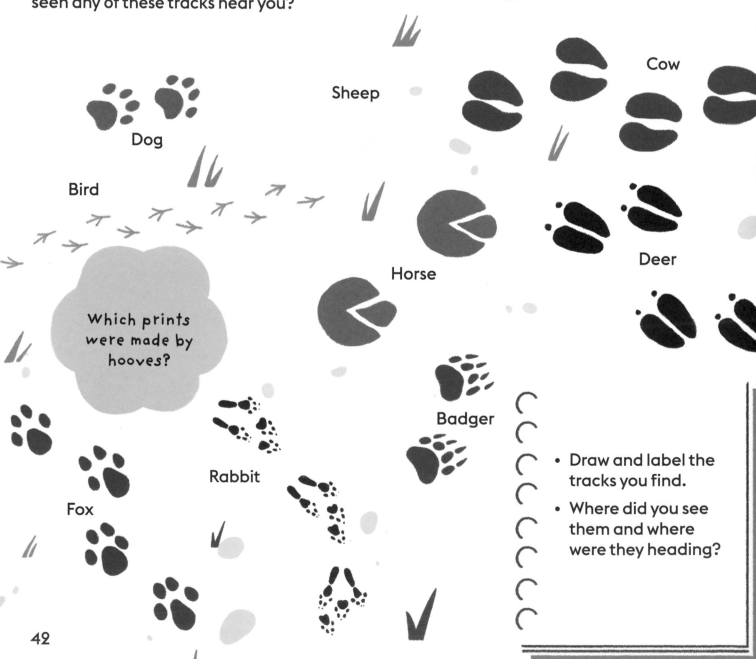

Duck

Cow

Sheep

Dog

Bird

Horse

Deer

Which prints were made by hooves?

Badger

Rabbit

Fox

- Draw and label the tracks you find.
- Where did you see them and where were they heading?

Animal Homes

- Look up in the trees for stick nests built by squirrels, called dreys.

- Search for birds' nests made from twigs, moss, or mud. Some birds nest in the hollows of trees.

- Look for holes dug in the ground. Rabbits, foxes, badgers, and many other animals live in underground burrows.

Wash your hands after touching things, and never pick up poo.

Creature Clues

Spot these signs that some animals leave.

Feathers on the ground, which fall from birds as they clean themselves.

Empty **nutshells** left by birds and squirrels.

Marks or scratches on logs and trees.

Fur and **wool** tangled on fences, or posts that animals scratch against.

Animal **droppings** on the ground.

Nibbled **leaves** made by caterpillars and other insects.

43

Water Fun!

In warm weather, it's fun to explore the [water life] in ponds and streams. You can even ha[ve a] splashy time in a puddle!

Always have a grown-up with you when you play near water.

Stay Safe Near Water!

- Wear rubber boots or plastic shoes—there may be sharp objects in the water.
- Wear waterproof trousers or take spare dry clothes.
- Never push anyone in.
- Never stand on frozen lakes or ponds.

You will need:

- A fishing net or a glass jar with string tied around the top
- A small bucket or bowl

Pond Dipping

1. Find a safe bank to sit on, or wade into shallow water that you can get in and out of easily.
2. Fill a bucket with pond water, then slowly drag your net or jar back and forth through the water.
3. Tip your catch into the bucket.
4. Can you name any of the creatures you find? Remember to put them back in the pond once you have examined them!

You will need:

- Rocks
- Sticks
- Stones and pebbles

Dam building

In a stream or river, water flows around rocks and boulders. Build a dam across a shallow section by adding sticks and stones. Can you stop the water from getting through?

Remember to remove the dam before you leave.

Use a long stick to measure how deep the water is before and after you make the dam.

Using a Map

Grab a map before you head off on an adventure and plan the best route to where you are going. A map could also help you discover some interesting things along the way!

Look at a map that you have at home or download one from the internet.

What's What?

Most maps have a key. This tells you what all of the lines and symbols on the map mean. Once you understand the symbols you can avoid having a picnic in a soggy field or camping in a parking lot!

Key

LAKE	POND	ROAD	FOOTPATH	RIVER	TREES	GRASSLAND	BRIDGE	RAILROAD

TRAIN STATION	BUS	PARKING LOT	VIEW POINT	CHURCH	HOSPITAL	SCHOOL	PICNIC AREA

How High?

The wavy lines on a map are contour lines. They show how flat or hilly the land is.

When there are no lines or they are wide apart, the land is flat.

When the lines are close together the land is steep.

A number in a circle tells you the height at the top of the hill or mountain.

How Far?

Everything on a map is shrunk down to fit on the paper. To find out how big and how far things really are, look at the scale bar.

This helpful scale helps us understand the relationship between the distance on a map and the distance on land.

240

| 0 | 1 | 2 |

km / mi

Draw Your Own Map

Draw a map of your area or your journey to school.

Add roads, paths, buildings, and green spaces.

Can you make up some map symbols of your own?

Draw contour lines for hills and slopes.

47

Pine Cone Feeders

In winter, there aren't many berries and bugs about for birds to eat. Make this feeder to give your feathered friends a seedy treat.

1. In a mixing bowl, stir together ½ a cup each of the bird seed, raisins, and lard or margarine.

2. Tie string around the cones, leaving a long end at the top to hang them with. Pack the seed mix around the cones.

3. Put the feeders in the fridge to harden. Hang them from a balcony or a tree in your garden and watch the birds come to feast.

You could also put a dish of water out for birds in the winter.

- How many different kinds of bird come to the feeders?
- Can you name them all?

Obstacle Course

Challenge your friends and family to complete a woodland obstacle course. Set up these activities to test their speed, strength, and sporting skills, or create some obstacles of your own.

Watch out for bumps and hidden holes that might trip you up.

In and Out

Lay a trail of sticks and stones along the ground. Competitors have to weave in and out as quickly as they can.

Over or Under

Balance a thin stick across the top of two logs or stones. Competitors must jump over or crawl under the stick without knocking it off.

Hang On

Find a tree with a strong, low-hanging branch. Competitors have to hang from the branch for as long as possible.

Step to It

Find some short, sturdy logs and space them out in a row. Make sure they don't wobble or topple over. Competitors have to step from one log to the next without falling off.

51

Tracking with Sticks

Head for some woods with a group of friends and play a game of hide-and-seek with sticks. Work in teams to leave a trail or be tracked down.

1. Collect lots of sticks, then get into two teams—Trackers and Trailers. Each team needs at least two people.

2. Choose a tree as base camp in the park or woods where you are playing. This is where everyone returns to.

3. The Trackers wait at base camp, shut their eyes, and count to 100 while the Trailers set off.

4. The Trailers lay a trail of sticks on the ground in the shape of arrows to point the way. They then hide and wait to be found.

5. The Trackers follow the arrows to discover their friends' hiding spot. Once discovered, the teams swap and the game starts again.

Try making these tracking signs with your sticks:

turn left

not this way

turn right

end of trail